# Ballylin

## Memories of Life
in a Small Irish Village

JOAN COMISKEY

This work presents my recollection of events. Some names, identifying details, and locales have been changed to protect the privacy of individuals.

BISAC Categories:
Biography & Autobiography/Personal Memoirs
Biography & Autobiography/Women

ISBN-13: 978-1494469122
ISBN-10: 149446912X

Printed in the United States of America
CreateSpace, Charleston, SC

Cover Photograph: Copyright ©Fotosearch.com
www.fotosearch.com

# for granny

who laughed with us, cried with us,
taught us to sing and to dance—
who cared for us, prayed for us, and
encouraged us to hope and to dream

# Memories

---

## *Early Years*

---

✤

# Ballylin

201-947-4675

Kevin,

Thanks

Joan Carniskey

early years

# hail morning

Growing up in rural Ireland, I was designated a sickly child — or, with Irish sensitivity, "delicate." My grandmother cared for me from infancy, and we shared a bed until I was a healthier nine-year old.

On awakening, Granny would step out of bed, remove her large nightgown, and instruct me "not to look until she was decent." As soon as she had put on a huge brassiere and a formidable corset with strings and suspenders, she stepped into very large, warm knickers, and then I was allowed to watch and to join in morning prayers.

As she put on her black dress, we prayed for the dead, then for the "poor souls in Purgatory." I envisioned Purgatory as a warm waiting room with very little light. I couldn't imagine a God who made you wait until small faults were healed, but I never said that. As she combed, braided, and pinned her long grey hair, Granny prayed always for a "special intention," but what it was was never voiced. My only role was to join in the prayers, not to ask questions, and to be as reverent as the cold air would permit. Prayers finished, Granny put on an apron over her black dress, picked up her glasses, and went downstairs to light the stove.

That morning ritual with Granny remains clear in my head, and, to this day, the memories from those mornings give me great comfort, especially in times of sorrow. I'm fairly sure that *I* was the "special intention."

# "insignificant" address

Our little village in southern Ireland in the 1930s boasted of a population of about 100. Its "insignificance" was marked for all to see by an entry in a local guidebook mentioning that this "area" was "on the road to Dublin," nothing more.

Our surroundings consisted of two groceries, one church, one school, one post office, eight public houses (pubs), and a police station. We bragged of our security being assured with one police sergeant and two guards. We also had a white sheepdog that had adopted the police and slept all day outside in the fresh air.

Most of the villagers were poor and farming was the only way to make a living for many. One or two owned small farms, but most were just farm hands. We had a garage where the owner repaired tractors. He also acted as driver for special events, usually funerals. The shoemaker saved shoes for as long as he could by clever stitching, but his alcohol use would often cause him to go on "benders," leaving his wife and five children to pray that all the shoes on the shelf would be repaired as he sobered, and they'd bring in badly needed income.

Few people owned or drove motorcars—and all were easily recognized. The parish priest and curate owned one each and an old lady from outside the village drove very slowly into our village once a month—so slowly that the kids ran beside the car encouraging her to "hurry up!" And our Uncle Leo owned a tiny, dilapidated jalopy that barely ran and which our mother wouldn't let us ride in—the car was too unreliable; we always fought over the seats; and Uncle Leo often stopped for a pint or two along the way.

The diversion of the day, when we were young, was the bus that went to Dublin 50 miles away three days a week. The bus stopped at the post office and, as kids, we watched as people (never more than two) boarded to spend the day in the big city—a place we always dreamt of.

Returning late at night, the bus brought us the evening paper—promised to our house, but delivered only after the bus driver and his helper had read all of it. Granny had the first "read," then our mother; finally we three girls got the comics. This small breath of "outside air" sustained us; any change in our routine energized us, and we missed the comics if they failed to show.

Church attendance was the highlight of village activities, and Sunday Mass was heavily attended. Confession on one Saturday every month was a procedure, and, in our case, a way to just leave the house, rather than an opportunity for "telling our sins."

Funerals were small. A horse-drawn hearse and a few mourners—not always friends of the deceased—walked to escort the departed to his or her final rest.

Weather was generally overcast, especially in fall and winter, and at times grey and depressing. But spring and summer in the village were always a joy for us children. We played outside in our large garden—where we were safely walled in and unable to wander away. We climbed trees, ran races, and played with our toys, always being glad to "teach class," all three being the pupil and teacher at different times. And our mother was as excited as we were when we all started to read, as reading was the only entertainment available to us besides the radio, much listened to, but, without electricity in the village, dependent on batteries.

Our travel was limited to occasional trips to a small market town six miles away. On those rare occasions when we *had* rides in a motorcar, we were sworn to behave and not to fight, and our mother would promise to take us to the "pictures" if we were good. Always persuasive and charming, she did not point out that the "pictures" were nine miles away and not an easy trip without a car.

For the most part, village life was peaceful, mundane, and predictable—and, for most young inhabitants, a stimulus to leave the village as soon as they were grown.

# a little "rest"

y mother, who had left my father in America shortly after my birth, brought me and my two sisters as infants and toddlers back to her native Ireland from Brooklyn. I'd like to think that there was no connection between the two events, but with two girls already in the family one-year apart, she needed a change.

My mother had long complained to my father of fatigue and stress and had finally suggested a "vacation" in Ireland—for a little "rest"—which she said would be good for her and us three girls, the youngest, me, being a problem with an allergy to milk.

And so, my mother returned to the small rural village she had left only eight years earlier in search of an exciting new life in America—just like the ones she saw romantically played out in "the pictures" with Claudette Colbert, Norma Shearer, Douglas Fairbanks, and John Barrymore.

On arriving in Ireland, we moved in with her mother—Granny—who owned one of the small "pub and groceries" in the village. The old, rather dowdy rooms behind and above the shop consisted of a kitchen with a fireplace, a dining room, a drawing room, and several bedrooms. There was no running water or electricity—only oil lamps for light. The rooms were always cool and damp—so damp that the wall paper was curled down away from the wall in spots in every room. There was a front door that led to both levels of the living area and a door at the back of the pub that led to the kitchen.

My mother's brother, our Uncle Leo, lived in the house, too, and helped Granny in the pub and shop. My mother's two sisters were both married (one with six children, the other childless) and lived some distance away.

Our breadwinner was Granny, a stern, hard-working woman who had had six children and, when we came to live with her, had already lost two sons and a husband.

Our family had little money to count on and we relied on the fairly small income brought in by the little pub and grocery, with Granny steadily trying to keep us all afloat. A savvy businesswoman, Granny was quick to send notices of bills due to those she knew could afford to pay. But, since cash in the village was hard to come by for many, Granny often simply wrote it "in the book" when people bought bread, tea, and butter at the shop. She was often rarely paid and patiently awaited "a few shillings a month" to meet her own needs.

Even as young children we knew our life depended on the generous hospitality of Granny, who loved us all very much. But Granny's one remaining son, Uncle Leo (who, at thirty one, planned to marry), would inherit the house and the little subsistence farm nearby upon Granny's death, as was the custom—leaving us to wonder where our living quarters would be if and when Granny died.

As we grew, my sisters and I were not aware of being *different*, but we were sometimes the objects of minor attention in the village — we were known to have been born in *Brooklyn*. Even though all three of us had come as infants/toddlers to live in Ireland, we were sometimes referred to as "Yanks."

Information about our father, Andrew, exiled in America, came only from our mother, and his name was rarely mentioned. Her version of the early short marriage was that our father could not hold a job; he drank at times; and had no ambition beyond the small apartment and life in Brooklyn. Any mention of him consisted of complaints of lack of financial support. "Your father never has sent a penny and he probably never will," she'd coldly state.

Her only reference to his general character was to say sharply "His only conversation was 'What's new?' when he met people." She said he was careless and dull. Often she spoke of a grey hat which was a permanent part of his wardrobe, which he refused to alter.

Once a month, for a short time, we saw letters from America; the contents were rarely shared. We knew enough not to pry, at least when we were too young to understand, but we sensed a tension whenever our father's name was mentioned. Some of the letters, we'd learn much later, carried gossipy, but untrue, tales about our father having an affair with a French woman; always hanging out in a bar; not working. These letters were often written by "friends" back in the Brooklyn neighborhood who were envious of our father's "new-found freedom" and "good luck" of being "relieved" of family responsibilities. Untruthful as the letters were, our mother took them all to heart and her bitterness only deepened.

References to our father thus always caused us discomfort, if not a little embarrassment. The unwritten rule seemed to be to avoid any mention of him, which would upset our mother, whose happiness we shared. To change her mood or cause her anguish left us torn and guilty.

As years slipped by, our mother's version of the story varied, and, as kids, we were at one time told of our father's death, a fact soundly contradicted when letters and a selection of favorite comics arrived addressed to us.

It was never made clear to us that our father hadn't expected his wife to leave him alone in America and not return. And, in her own way, Granny kept the connection to our father always in the back of our minds. One of her favorite pronouncements was, "You will all go to America when you grow up. You will see your father." But, living as we were then, as three very young girls in a small Irish village, America appeared to exist on another very far-away planet.

For now, however, in spite of an uncertain future, a lack of steady income, and wonderings about our father, we were content in our home. Our childhood in the village was a happy one—with laughter, play, music, and much love all around us.

# shampoo

ashing your hair could be quite a procedure in a house without central heat or running water. In our early years, an announcement was required before the procedure could start.

Granny would say, "We'll wash your hair today," and a large stove fire would be laid. The turf (coal) would be stacked and care taken to build a big fire early in the morning. Large saucepans of water would take hours to warm up and finally to heat. We had a large china basin in one of the bedrooms and an adult would carry it downstairs to the kitchen.

It was necessary to shed heavy sweaters and be partially naked before plunging one's head into the water. Due to cold surroundings, this proved to be a slow process. As girls, we hated to undress — or, as we heard it, "to strip." Modesty was not the only deterrent; frigid air formed a large part of our reluctance.

Shampoo for hair was expensive and, in spite of our protests, considered a luxury. We settled for the dreaded "yellow soap" — a large bar of industrial-strength cleanser used for sheets, tables, and all types of household cleaning. It was unscented and should have been softened before application. However, Granny, who often did the hair-washing, believed a strong hand and a hard rub would not hurt. We were frightened of putting our heads into the washbowl. Our delaying tactics consisted of cries of "It's too hot!" or "It's too cold!," necessitating addition of water of either temperature to correct the condition. We tried to keep a small piece of dry towel available to save us from the dreaded "soap in my eyes" syndrome.

Soap stung and temporarily felt painful, but we had learned to exaggerate plaintively, and cries of "I'm blind!" or "Blinded!" could be heard from the depths of the warm bowl. A strong hand pressed down on each head. Granny had washed too many heads in her time to be gentle with ours. Her touch was firm, managerial, and would brook no resistance. I had the least problem, having lost my hair to ringworm at an early age, which left me with fine thin hair, easily washed. My older sister Mona shared my fate (minus ringworm), and was in and out of the basin in minutes. The middle sister, Patricia, however, had massive curls and dreaded these ablutions, knowing "tangles" would follow.

Hair combing following a shampoo could be painful, as hair would form knots and needed to be combed out. Patricia, of the curly-thick locks, endured much as a large comb was pulled through her hair. We fine-haired sisters "dried out"' in a short time and stood damp — but secretly triumphant — as Patricia howled in protest. Hair was combed flat; no attempt to curl the uncurly or shape the shapeless; you were clean.

However, you could not leave the house or indeed the confines of the kitchen if you had a "wet head." Everyone "knew" there could be dire consequences of leaving heat and going outside. Threats included tuberculosis, with apparently rapid onset following hair washing. And then there was deafness. A Mrs. Glendillon of the village lost her hearing because "she went outside with a wet head." We often saw her riding her bicycle to and from work—stone deaf—wondering how she avoided the cars and trucks around her. And, of course, hair washing during menstruation carried dire warnings—unspecified, but enough of a threat implied to suggest terminal illness or even insanity. It was no use trying to make connections—if you had a "wet head" and went out, chills, fever, and invalidism would surely follow.

Keeping three pre-adolescents inside for hair drying proved a challenge for Granny for at least an hour.

# sewing Lady

er name was Lydia Gorman. She was our seamstress. Indeed, when we were young, she was the only seamstress in the village. Lydia shortened our dresses, sewed our coats, and could reline worn skirts so they could be handed down from older to younger child.

Lydia's skills were important to us. Our mother was not a sewer. In fact, she proudly proclaimed her lack of sewing ability, "I don't sew or mend"—a boast greatly increasing her already low status with her two sisters. It was not enough that she had left a husband in America and had come back home with three very small children. Now there was but another fault added to a long list.

Lydia lived at the end of the village, a short walk from our home. We liked to visit her since she never left the house and had a slight air of mystery on that account—and she was a Protestant, a rarity in our village where just about everyone was Catholic. She had a brother, Patrick, a taciturn, disagreeable soul who did not enjoy children or grown-ups.

Patrick had once worked in the Post Office and it was rumored that he had purloined money over the years. The story—with variations—ran that he had opened mail and forged signatures to cash the checks enclosed. We never had proof of these "sins"; in fact, even then, we wondered who in our small village would be *receiving* checks in the mail. We rarely received money, mailed or otherwise, and very few inhabitants had check books or even knew of a bank.

Facts not withstanding, Patrick's reputation was permanently tainted. He never spoke of his "sins" and no one could approach him on the subject. Lydia, we were sure, also suffered from this cloud of suspicion.

Sitting in Lydia's house, although the occupants were of great interest to us, was an early version of our idea of Purgatory. We waited; we were measured; and then Lydia approached us with an array of pins — which, in horror, I expected would be applied to my body, but which, with great relief, were actually for the cloth she was working with. We had to stand still for what seemed to us, hours. Poor Lydia tried to divert us with stories. Her voice was soft and gentle.

One day, when I had been particularly restless and more than usually obnoxious, she stunned me with a simple statement. "You know," she said, "I learned to sew in prison." She paused, allowing my jaw to drop, and rapidly pinned more material near my knees. I was stunned, unsure how to proceed, but fascinated. "For how long?," my voice quavered, partly in sympathy, but also wanting to continue the conversation.

"I was in jail for two years," she replied softly, "and my brother for ten. We were accused." She waited, wanting to hear if I could fathom the word; I didn't question it, so she proceeded.

"We were charged with stealing money from the Post Office." I was moved, enthralled, and shocked; in a moment all rumors had been confirmed. As usual I was accompanied by an older sister, but she was reading and literally had not heard a word. Even I knew you didn't interrupt a confession; some vague instinct bade me be still and wait. Pinning my shoulder, she said, "It was very hard for me; I was in a big room all day sewing, and at night in a small cell with just a bed and a small table. They wouldn't let me even read my Bible."

I remembered that Lydia was a Protestant—big unknown capitals in my mind. I knew that not all people were of the Roman Catholic faith. I knew their belief was in God, but in my mind, not in the Blessed Virgin. I had grown up with the Blessed Mother and Baby Jesus and the bloody end in flogging and crucifixion. In all honesty, I did not understand the differences; everyone went to heaven. Some people were in a waiting room called Purgatory, but apart from the capital P of the other religion, I was totally ignorant.

Lydia apparently decided that that was the end of her story. She removed the pins and told me to come back in a week. I went home, and during the evening I thought of poor Lydia's past. Prison was unknown to me; I had seen pictures of Fagin, the condemned man in *Oliver Twist* and he looked desperate, dark and frightening. I had not shared Lydia's tale with my sisters or my family at home. I felt I had somehow stumbled on a forbidden topic and should not have heard her story, and, therefore, should not repeat it.

Eventually, as Lydia's eyesight began failing and my mother decided she wanted someone cheaper, we found, outside the village, a small lady who designed and made coats. She endeared herself to our mother by sewing three coats from a vile green material she had overstocked.

Lydia Gorman slipped out of our lives and eventually passed away — but I imagine her happily ensconced in a well-lit Paradise, sewing angels' wings when they are torn.

# elizabeth

My earliest memory of my mother, Elizabeth, was of her standing in front of a mirror in her slip, a slim young girl in her early twenties pencilling in her eyebrows. In our low-key house, this was almost a decadent image, exciting and even naughty. I was sure no other child saw such a sight on awakening since no women in our area wore make-up.

We adored, and even as kids, protected our mother who seemed to us to be frail and sometimes younger than we were. We knew early on not to burden her with cuts, vomit, or tears in our clothing. She seemed to need our constant reassurance and at times to need to get away from us; trips to Dublin were often a chance for her to shop or see a movie. We were always nervous until she returned safely to be there for all three of us.

Her main focus in our upbringing, as far as we could see, seemed to be to teach us good dining manners. As very young kids we ate in the kitchen when there were visitors at the table in the dining room. Our envy and huge curiosity were keen, but we were kept from the "grown up" table until our manners met the criteria set by our master teacher. As we grew older we learned to sit "nicely" at table, to say grace, and to wait to have bread and butter passed to us, instead of our reaching out and grabbing as had been our custom. After a few faulty starts, we all joined the guests (rare, and thus important). We waited until spoken to before speaking and held back from the special treats at table until the older folks had tasted, and we restrained ourselves from fighting with one another. I recall learning to eat apple pie (known as tart to us) with a fork, a skill which took much practice in my case.

My mother had developed good taste while away in America; even a simple dress looked stylish when she wore it with a plain scarf or a touch of white at the collar. Her hair was often styled (she visited the local hair dresser routinely, always managing to scrape together the necessary funds), and her makeup was always discreet, but effective. She was a sharp contrast to her sisters—the one with six children being "too busy" to care for costume changes, and the childless one, who tended to plain clothes and, at least in her visits to us, seemed to dress down and carry an air of suffering and disapproval like a cloak.

My mother's family insisted on calling her "Betty," but she hated the familiar short version, preferring to be called "Elizabeth," to her a more elegant name. Her sisters were always envious of her and at times openly hostile to her. Even in our early years we sensed the hostility and were keenly aware of the sly, and often not so sly, digs sent in her direction. The sisters felt that "Betty" had the best of both worlds—sailing to America at an early age, marrying, and then leaving her husband and arriving home with three noisy girls who relied on others for their care.

We three youngsters learned to be wary of visiting relatives — references were often made to our huge good fortune in having a place to live and a Grandmother to feed and clothe us. We were well aware of these facts, and sensing some censure in the comments, refrained from pointing out our helplessness over any of these realities. Besides, learning "good manners" included listening to our elders and making small talk about the weather and the health or illness of older people, not arguing back.

The whole effect was to present three well-brought-up young girls who had learned the art of listening, but also of hiding their true feelings behind small talk.

Our mother was often ill as we grew up; she developed pleurisy and was hospitalized several times while we were children. Her absence was a great trial to all of us, but our older sister, Mona, felt it most. Always emotionally insecure, she cried constantly and was hard to reassure; few words would comfort her, and as we could not visit the hospital (run by, to us, demon, dragon-like nuns), her grief kept all of us tense until the return of the patient. And Granny had already been devastated by the loss of two of her sons, which made the frequent hospitalizations of her daughter even more threatening.

Our mother eventually recovered fully, but she was not above using her past illness to lead a semi-invalid life when daily living became too much to bear. She stayed late in bed and, as we began to attend school, we learned how to carry her tray upstairs with a light breakfast before leaving the house.

Whenever tensions arose, our mother could faint in a dramatic manner without seeming cause and never for long periods, creating an effect on observers which we children both feared and admired.

As we reached adolescence, our mother adopted varying attitudes toward us, at times seeming to be our age and joining in make-up trials and clothing style choices. As we learned to use make-up more often, however, she became overprotective, adding to our confusion. We learned to avoid scenes, keeping plans secret, and using one another as conspirators when needed.

Our mother, it seems, was always longing for a better life outside the confines and narrowness of our small village. She had searched for it once in America, but returned home unfulfilled. This time her dream was to move to Dublin with Granny and us three girls to be close to shopping and the movies.

# still voices

onversation in the pub and grocery tended to be predictable. Bar talk consisted of snatches of greetings; rarely more than two or three words. "Bad day" from one tired farmer about to sip his first stout. "Ah 'twas" would be the simple response from another weary farmer about to escape into a fresh pint, badly needed.

The shop was divided into a grocery area at the entrance, then, to the right, a small partitioned bar. The wood was old and there were benches attached to the partition. One or two bar stools were strategically placed, but rarely used by patrons. Whether from habit or custom, or to facilitate a quick exit, most patrons liked to stand at the bar.

One regular customer would always call out, "Anything strange or startling?" as he entered. No one would respond, since nothing of either sort occurred. Others would offer a brief and often peremptory greeting, "You'll have the rain," surely a prescient comment. Our climate was well known to all; rain came almost daily.

Climate played a large part in the atmosphere of our small village. Summers were bright and we often had sun-filled days. Autumn was melancholy, but still dry. Winter, however, came in early with dark evenings and very few lights, except for oil lamps in the windows. Dampness was common. If the rain came, it could be constant and chilled. We rarely had white snow covering our trees. The result was a long, damp, dark season where a lighted pub with the warmth of bodies provided a beacon for the inhabitants.

Drawn as to a lighthouse, weary men who had toiled all day on small farms or had driven cattle to a fair or fed chickens or pigs were drawn to the light to relieve the tedium. Many a customer had a mother-in-law at home. Some had sick, complaining wives; almost all had three or four children anxious to be fed and washed, and life for most was contained in a small smoky cottage.

The darkness often prevented the small fights that sometimes took place in the backyard of the pub. It was hard to fight when you could barely see your opponent. "Hold a light," somebody once called, "so I can see to hit him."

During the war, the quality of talk changed nightly. President Roosevelt's voice was familiar to us because of the radio, and his courage was admired. Even the old enemy, England, had a strong person. Mr. Churchill, who although not a fan of the Irish, gave strong, literate speeches, and was quoted frequently. Hitler was designated the Antichrist and the bar talk was full of foreboding. Some patrons believed that Germans would parachute into Dublin and march through the countryside occupying, ravaging, and taking over.

Mr. DeValera, our president at the time, gave long, hawkish-sounding speeches, mostly not understood as he persisted in using Irish—a language the elders did not know and we younger students were struggling to master. "Dev," however, provoked some discussion and occasional hostility between the old Fianna Fail versus Fine Gael political parties.

Friday or Saturday nights' conversations were a dramatic change. Voices were louder, spirits higher, money flowed more freely. Sometimes a verse or two of old poems were recited. Someone always recited Joyce Kilmer's "Trees." Another favorite was "The boy stood on the burning deck," with prompts from listeners where needed.

Stories would be told on Saturday nights if the mood was right. One involved the "Banshee," a local witch-figure of gloomy portent who combed long hair and presaged death in the family. Stories of a black dog were also chilling; a vision of such an animal also indicated a catastrophe or a death in the family.

The bar area itself was not equipped for storytelling; such occasions required a trip to the "snug," a small room at the back of the pub. This, generally, was a place of privilege for women who wanted a drink but did not want to sit or stand at the bar with the men. During the day, sometimes a few women would have a small sherry or a glass of port wine after a funeral or in preparation for a big day's shopping in the city. But at night, the "snug" was the perfect place for storytelling. There was a smelly, smoky fire in the grate and the murky atmosphere added to the gloom of the surroundings.

I did not realize at my early age that I was learning a little Shakespeare on these nights. Some of the "snug" storytellers told of a "knocking" that occurred before a death in the family. We didn't know the origin, but the phrase

"There'll be a death in the house; I heard a knocking" was familiar to me long before *Macbeth* became part of my reading.

# Old Friend

Dermot O'Malley came to our pub when I was about seven or eight. The bar was the reason for his visit, although he was an old friend. He was selling a pony and led the animal to the door hoping to tie him there while he had a drink. Granny, wise to the "drop in for a quick drink" trick (knowing he'd really stay for seven or eight), insisted that he find someone to hold the pony while he drank.

It was a busy day, and Granny was called to serve drinks. I stood shyly at the door watching people. Although I was a small, lightly-boned child, Dermot gave me the reins and said, "Hold this, I'll be back in five minutes."

He left me with the reins attached to a large animal. I was petrified, but slightly flattered to be trusted. My older, sisters were not around; I grieved at this. I wanted to show off. I had been chosen, after all, to control this large wild beast.

The horse stood quietly, his large eyes looked sad. I felt I could pet him, but I was too nervous to actually touch him. It seemed hours, but it was probably only a few moments later, that Granny called to me: "Come inside; it's getting cold." Proudly, I called out: "I can't! I'm holding the horse for Dermot!"

Horrified, she flew over to the bar and practically dragged a reluctant Dermot to the door. "Leaving this little girl alone with this big animal, Derry. What were you thinking?," she scolded him."Finish your drink and take your horse and go home."

Dermot smiled sheepishly, slipped me a half-crown, and said, "You did good," before taking the reins away. He left soon and I reveled in my triumph and in my money, not to be shared, since I alone had earned it.

Two years later, there was a murder in a place called Wolfhill, not far from our village. A bank manager, carrying a large sum of money was shot dead on his way home on a country road. We were unaccustomed to murder; the papers revelled in the story. I read all the details with fascination. My mother did not discuss the case in our presence; too much violence; "you're too young" was her reason. Some weeks into the murder investigation, there was an arrest made. Granny spoke in low tones to my mother; but in our presence, no name was said. The newspaper was hidden; all my powers of excavation failed to help me find it.

Finally, the radio began to tell the tale of the murder. One morning the announcer related the arrest and possible future execution of the killer. It was a local man. In fact, the murderer had been photographed "assisting the police" early in the case. The man was married, a farmer, and well known to the locals. His name was Dermot O'Malley. I was stunned, horrified, and at the same time, a little elated. I had privileged, personal knowledge of a killer. I could brag to my two sisters of my act of kindness years earlier. I had held the horse (by now a huge beast in my imagination) and been praised and paid by a killer.

Our family was devastated by the arrest. The subsequent trial was followed with great attention and, when the guilty verdict came in, Granny wept all day. I had not known that one of her dead sons had gone to school and played rugby with the killer. We were, therefore, linked even more closely to the tragedy than I first assumed.

Dermot had requested that an old school friend, now a priest, attend him at his execution. My excitement changed to chill and finally horror as the execution was carried out in six months. Our bar was filled with locals and the murder and trial were debated every night. I listened whenever I could be invisible and overlooked. I never spoke of my acquaintance with poor Dermot. Sometimes the horse appeared in my dreams, not sad or patient as he had been, but large, stamping and threatening. Dermot himself was never in the dream.

# prayer book

ranny's prayer book stayed on the hall stand all the time. It was leather-bound and full of clippings, notes in her own writing, and memorial cards for the dead. I became well acquainted with it as a young child when it was given to me to keep me quiet during Mass. I found Mass long and tiring — the priest had his back to all of us, spoke Latin, and the only highlight was the ringing of the bell at the consecration.

I leafed through the book, reading the memorial cards, yellowed with age. There was an old, folded telegram packed in the pages. I opened it always with great care, afraid to break any of it. It said "Mother after dying," and the date was so long ago I marveled at its survival. To think Granny had had a mother mystified me. She was already old to me (probably in her early seventies) — grey haired, clad in black, knew everything, and, after all, had had six children.

The prayer cards fascinated me. Most had pictures of the deceased. There were young women and men, with tender references made to their early passing. "Devoted Wife," "Loving Child," "Dedicated Priest." Some contained unfamiliar phrases, but the prayers touched me.

There were press clippings, many for bragging purposes. A great-grand nephew graduated as a "chartered accountant" and went early to Hong Kong. A grandchild passed her Leaving Certificate and graduated. A marriage took place far away, unattended by any of the family, but described as "fashionable," "attended by many notables," "celebrated by a Bishop," "attended by Fathers," and, with great pride, "of the Jesuit order." But there were other clippings as well. I did not discuss the clippings; I knew that I was prying in a private area and could be barred from it.

At the back of the prayer book were several handwritten pages — verses Granny had liked and carefully copied. Most of them spoke of grief and loss. The prayers, obviously favorites with Granny because the pages were so used, became familiar to me. "Prayers for a happy death." "After Communion." "In time of loss." "For a special intention." Cards with "a relic of St. Teresa, the Little Flower" (with a piece of wood from her coffin embedded in the card). "Prayer to St. Jude" (extremely popular in Ireland as Patron of Hopeless Cases, e.g., drink). "Prayer for travelers." "St. Christopher." Every aspect of life was covered by these serene-faced saints who know all the secrets of survival.

"The Thirty Days Prayer," a special blue insert, contained a prayer to be said every day for thirty days. I did not fathom the connection with the number 30, but it was vital to the prayerful that not one day be missed. The "Thirty Days Prayer" was for large intentions — imminent births, vocations, long illnesses of dubious outcome. Granny was devoted to the prayer, and often recommended it to friends.

During my childhood perusal of the prayer book, I found a little lock of blond hair in an envelope. I did not dare to ask, but assumed it came from the head of one of her sons. The hair — blond, shining, and amazingly smooth after all those years — brought to mind a small bright-eyed boy whom I may have seen in an old picture.

Granny rarely missed Mass and the prayer book was almost exclusively for the Sunday ceremony. Once, when she was confined to bed, she called downstairs, "Bring me my prayer book," and I carried it upstairs. I stayed with her — not because of religious fervor — but I feared the call intimated her immediate demise, unspeakable as that thought was. I wanted to be close.

# Breakfast for the priests

nce a month in the parish there was a special Mission Mass during which both the pastor (the parish priest) and curate (his young assistant just "learning the ropes") said Mass and heard confessions — both before and after the service. (On the other Sundays, either the pastor or the curate came to the village, but not both together.) The Mission Mass was an occasion to check on the villagers for attendance at Mass, to visit the sick, and, if necessary, to speak to "troubled" parishioners. (And of those there always seemed to be many.) There were no secrets in our little village. Men who drank too much were seen and noticed. Wives who were unhappy stayed married, but voiced dissatisfaction to close friends. Young men stayed in bed on Sundays and avoided confession lest their "wild" outings be stopped by admonitions from the priests.

The curate, a small, sallow, sarcastic priest, was in charge of visiting the "sinners." One of the local girls had the misfortune of two pregnancies out of wedlock. She had been refused communion on one occasion and had had several visits from the curate, presumably to remind her of eternal damnation ahead.

We youngsters, however, did not have any real concept of the sweeping menu of sins at that age, and they did not faze us. We had been taught to obey our elders, not to fight with one another, and never to steal, or to kill anyone. To us, fighting and stealing were the only sins we had to cope with.

Our house had been chosen to provide the breakfast for these two priests after their labors. The preparation took at least one week. We had a special tablecloth that was washed, starched, and ironed. Special cups, usually left in a closet in the living room, were carefully washed and dried. We young people could not touch this "special china" for the priests. They were treated almost like the chalice on the altar.

The meal consisted always of bacon, eggs, toast, a large pot of strong tea (the pastor liked his tea with a kick in it), brown bread baked fresh, as well as a white loaf, and, if possible, a side of soda bread. The pastor liked his bacon crisp and insisted that the bacon rinds be left on — he chewed noisily on them as he talked. The curate was a poor eater; he was chronically pale and had a digestive problem. He could not eat bacon and liked his eggs firm, with the yolk unbroken. My mother served the meal, but Granny had always prepared it and hovered nearby, ready to greet the two priests.

As children we were kept out of the way; hidden in the kitchen or playing in the yard so as not to make noise. As we grew older, I remember always racing through the dining room in my bathrobe trying to reach the kitchen without being seen. The pastor would be reading the *Independent* and often missed my run through the room. The curate, who seemed to have extra-sensory hearing, always embarrassed me by calling out, "Good morning. Aren't you saying hello to your pastor?" — leaving me awkward and feeling naked, although I was fully covered by the robe.

Granny loved the pastor and was wary of the curate's sharp tongue. She would wait until he left the room to make one of his "visits" to sinners and then run in to relate a story or juicy piece of gossip to the old man. He was quite deaf, so her tidbits could be heard clearly by all. But she enjoyed her moment and never really revealed startling news.

The curate liked to exit through our small bar instead of the rarely-used front door. His walk-through would cause early drinkers to drop their caps and mutter "Good day to you Father," hoping he would not comment on their early need for a pint. He'd smile sardonically and would identify each poor soul by name. "Hello Billy. How's the wife? How many children are there now? I didn't see you at confession today; I'm hearing again in an hour." Visible relief showed when he exited the main part of the shop and climbed into his beautiful car.

The pastor did not return to the church for confessions; his hearing loss caused great alarm to the locals so his "line" outside the box was short compared to the curate's. His disconcerting habit of shouting, "You *what*?" from the recesses of the confessional caused muffled laughter, as did his, "Who the hell are *you*?," which sent younger penitents into helpless giggles. The curate by comparison had a steady stream of penitents and disposed of all in a short time. Older parishioners would sometimes say, "I want to go back to when I was seven, Father," to which he would crisply reply, "Well I don't. Tell your sins and I'll absolve you; and go home."His strictness appealed to the locals; they struggled with both fear and admiration, thinking that when the old priest died, the curate would surely take over.

The curate was a superb preacher; his sermons were brief, to the point, and sometimes witty; always pungent. The parish priest, however, rambled on and people slept quietly in their hard seats until he finished. He became more acerbic as he aged and often struck the altar boys if they missed the bell for the consecration or forgot the wine at the offertory. "Hurry up you eegit" would sound from the altar, and the unfortunate altar boy would stumble up the steps, spilling wine and water around him.

Breakfast for the priests and the monthly Mission Mass continued for many years and ended when the parish priest died, and quite soon after, the curate.

# still life

arry Hovenden died on a chilly January morning. News of his death came to our house within a few hours. A local woman, who was involved with births and deaths, had prepared the body and reported the passing to our family. My mother was assigned to attend the wake, and, as the youngest child, aged eight, I was delegated to accompany her. My older sisters had learned the art of resisting such tasks, and their excuses were usually accepted. I had yet to learn the art of acceptable refusal. However, I was, in fact, very pleased to attend Harry's wake.

I remembered Harry well. He was a local farmer who allowed us to ride on his cart when he went to collect stacks of hay from his field. I remembered strong brown hands holding the reins; he never pulled on the horse, and was always gentle. When we arrived at the hay field, he was ready to help us. With those strong capable hands, he placed us three excited young girls far from the loading area. We rode back to our village on the back of the slide, thrilled to be part of the day's work. For a long time, we three sisters acted as if the hay rides carried us to foreign places.

Wakes were held in the home in most cases. The body, laid simply on a bed, was not embalmed or enhanced in any way. A religious brown tunic was placed over the torso and Rosary beads were entwined through the fingers of both hands. Harry's corpse was no exception.

I was unafraid to view a dead man; wakes were quite familiar to us. I must have seen many, even as a young child. Harry's, however, was special, and I was struck by the now waxen hands — hands I had often watched with admiration.

One of the mourners cried, "What happened to your lovely color, Harry?" People were shocked or amused. I echoed the question. The serene face on the lifeless, waxen figure draped in brown on the small bed looked like Harry fast asleep, except for the pallor. I felt he could awaken at any moment. My mother and I knelt at the side of the bed and prayed. Then she sprinkled holy water on the remains and we moved to the small kitchen off the bedroom.

It was the custom to claim that the deceased had gone to a "better place" and that God had called him or her to a "promised land." I wondered, "Did Harry get to drive a horse, and make hay stacks in that great farm in the sky?" No one told me animals were exempt from heavenly rewards, so I assumed that a horse could be provided. I hoped those strong, gentle brown hands could still be of use. Surely God would allow Harry to care for other children wherever Heaven was. I was sure we would meet again.

# Lily of the Valley

he strongly perfumed flower, Lily of the Valley, was a favorite of my mother's and lasted only briefly into the month of May. A usually happy sign of spring, the little white flower took on a different association and superstition in our family, one that we all later carried into adulthood.

Our much loved Uncle Leo, the only male living in our house, was tall and, to us, quite handsome. He had alternately teased and punished us as we grew and found troubles to get into. But in October one year, he became ill and took to his bed.

We children were unaware of his diagnosis and, at first, entertained him in his bedroom, bringing food from the kitchen while our mother "tidied" his bed and gave him local gossip. It was her idea to curtail our visits; the rooms were cold in the winter and, although a fire was lit, the sickroom was becoming somewhat more subdued.

Over the winter and into early spring, the uncle we loved became frail and quiet. We were banned from his room and became accustomed to doctors' visits and the unnerving sight of Granny weeping in a corner of the house when she left the sickroom.

In May, my mother brought Lily of the Valley into the room. The perfume filled the house and replaced the slight odor of illness that even we were observing.

One day soon after, my sister Patricia and I were summoned. We were told we were being sent to the "Aunts" for a few weeks. The "Aunts" were three of Granny's sisters, unmarried and quite comfortable in a nearby town. Our older sister, Mona, was sent to another Aunt who had several sons. (Mona, always the rebel, had refused to stay with "the Aunts" — having disobeyed their rules and broken some dishes on a previous visit.)

My sister and I left with some anticipation; we enjoyed the Aunts, knew the house well, and learned to "hide out" upstairs and read old American magazines. One of the Aunts had a bond with us; she took care of our meals, took us on long walks, and made us laugh with her loud voice and her overuse of rouge that gave her a merry look, like a circus clown's.

The other two Aunts were unusually quiet on this visit. We noticed how tolerant they were. Bedtime was not as strict as our previous visits and the general air was of sympathy and support for us.

One morning, two weeks into our visit, our favorite Aunt told us that "God had called Uncle Leo in the night." I, a pious nine-year-old, wondered how God "called" someone — By name? And how did one answer?

We were driven home a few days later. Arriving home, we found the house unusually quiet and blinds drawn in most of the windows. Our mother appeared all in black, looking beautiful. We still did not grasp what caused the change.

Going upstairs to change, we passed through our Uncle's room. It was stripped bare of all furniture and a new mattress was in place. No flowers seemed to be in the house. We noticed instead a slightly disinfectant smell, as if the room had been aired and scrubbed, as indeed it had.

The cause of Uncle Leo's death was tuberculosis, a highly contagious disease. The local Board of Health had insisted on "fumigating" the entire house and keeping children out of the house to avoid spreading the disease.

Our house was gloomy for some months. The loss was extremely hard on Granny; she had already lost two younger sons. Uncle Leo was her last. Neighbors and religious friends tried to comfort her, comparing her son to Christ, both having died at the age of 33. This was a statement of consolation and sympathy frequently used in those days, and it probably afforded some small measure of comfort to those grieving.

Lily of the Valley became associated with death in our family and a symbol of remembrance of the dearly departed. My mother never lost her affection for the flower nor her somber recollection of a loss suffered so long ago.

Granny kept cuttings from the newspapers of her son's death in her prayer book, nestled among the list of prayers for the dead used every Sunday.

# village medical men

As a child, it seemed to me that doctors appeared in the village out of nowhere, and I had learned to fear the medical profession early on. When I was very small, a doctor treated my ear infection with some very painful procedures. Therefore, it was with little pleasure that I observed the arrival of any new doctor who came to care for us in the village.

To me, these men picked our village to annoy and worry us. Later I learned that they were appointed by the Health Department. Often they were new graduates, but in one or two cases, they were men who had survived dubious pasts, and in some cases, faced uncertain futures.

When a doctor was assigned to the village, he first had to find a place to stay and then he "set up shop" in the local "dispensary" (clinic)—our name for a poorly-equipped room in a building near the police station stocked with a smelly disinfectant (known locally as "Jeyes Fluid"), carbolic soap, and rusty instruments.

The first new doctor I observed was a rather stiff, well-dressed man who administered our required diphtheria, tetanus, and small pox injections. I don't remember being hurt, but I can display the scars today. He treated the villagers like uneducated clods. They reciprocated by laughing at an embarrassing disaster he experienced. He decided to take up riding lessons and, on one occasion, his horse bolted and he had to walk home through the village carrying his bowler hat and riding crop. As the villagers saw it, only the Protestant English rode horses. The villagers used horses to plough the crops and draw carts to and from the fields. This elegant doctor left shortly after the riding incident.

Soon after, we were visited by another new doctor, Dr. Short, who arrived late one night in a rented car. He chose our pub as his first stop, needing perhaps the solace of a drink and some information about the village. Granny told him of the local digs for rent which were nearby. He purchased a bottle of whiskey and left before she could also tell him that his potential landlady, Lizzie, was the local midwife who also prepared bodies for burial. She had no medical training and hated doctors — who were, after all, a threat to her thriving private practice. The rooms at Lizzie's were cold and the house was full of drafts. It was not the least bit comfortable.

Dr. Short failed to appear in the "Dispensary" for a whole week, and Lizzie took the opportunity to be in charge. When he finally appeared, he looked terrible; he wore a long black coat and did not remove a large black hat even while seeing patients.

"The Doctor," as he was called in the village, became quite a familiar figure in our pub. He did not drink in public, but bought bottles of whiskey and had Granny wrap the bottles in a large brown paper bag, usually with a loaf of bread and a few sausages. He claimed that Lizzie served only boiled cabbage and that her skills were more dreadful in the kitchen than in the clinic. Granny formed a liking for this troubled being and even forgave him a bounced check or two.

One day, in a fit of passing sobriety, he asked if he could take us three children for a walk in the fields for exercise. We loved being taken for a walk, and our world had few men in it so we were thrilled with any attention. He talked about health, inspected our teeth, measured our height, and told us to be healthy so we could marry and have lots of children. We hoped to hear the secret of where babies came from, but, alas, no information ever came.

He did, however, lend us a large bundle of Charles Dickens' books. We did not tell him our reading was not up to Charles Dickens, but we loved the sketches, especially in *Oliver Twist.* We were both repelled and fascinated at the sight of Fagin in the condemned man's cell. The pictures became a magnet whenever we wanted a thrill — so we screamed and held one another for comfort.

Dr. Short soon lost interest in us. He became isolated in his miserable digs; he wrote long letters to Granny telling of cruel conditions in his life with Lizzie Condron. There was a leak in the roof and he claimed he had to hold an umbrella over himself before falling asleep. One day he left abruptly, no good-byes. He took a rented car to a nearby town and presumably went to a new place.

A month later, we were "blessed" by a new doctor. This medical man was the son of a local farmer. He was quiet, understanding, and willing to work in the village while awaiting a practice vacancy in a wealthier town nearby. Dr. Drake won hearts by buying drinks in our pub when he came to view the village and inspect the Dispensary.

One day, Dr. Drake came to our house when Mona, in bed with German measles, insisted on a visit from the "new" doctor. Mona fell in love at once. Her devotion may have helped to save my life, or at least to avoid acute discomfort on my part. Leaving her room, he was told that I was in bed with a tummy ache at the other end of the house.

Escorted by my mother, he came into the room, checked me for a fever, examined my tummy, and found a sore spot I had failed to notice. Dr. Drake diagnosed appendicitis. It brought attention to me and I was fussed over and became the center of attention in the house in a short time. To my dismay, the diagnosis was accurate and an emergency. I ended up in the operating room at the hospital many miles away within two hours. The surgeon assured me that Dr. Drake had indeed saved my life. My family instantly adopted him and would have killed the fatted calf if we owned one.

It occurs to me now that we never thought of a doctor's bill; I never recall his being paid. The tradition in the village was to give the doctor a bottle of whiskey or a brace of ducks, chickens, or even rabbits as payment.

Following Dr. Drake's departure, the Board of Health built a house for the doctors assigned to us. It stood close to the village and was quite modern. The occupants came from the north of Ireland, Kerry, and the midlands; all reasonable, intelligent and accomplished men, few, however, having the background of the early "pioneers."

Over the years I have met many other medical people, but none were like Dr. Short, the mysterious, seriously impaired man who brought us literature and reading as a pathway to learning and an interest in expanding our world.

# unheard melodies

acuum cleaner noise and a voice raised in song. I lay in bed awaiting these sounds that indicated an awakening of the rest of the occupants. As an eight-year-old niece, I had been sent "on vacation" by the family (Granny as the leader) to bring companionship to a childless aunt for a week. The family's view was that Aunt Eileen would enjoy the company of a small child as a distraction to an unnamed "unhappiness."

Aunt Eileen and her husband, Uncle John, lived in a large home some distance from us. I was awed by the clean, shining, almost sterile kitchen. The garden was well kept; the rooms upstairs shone and the floors were carpeted. Coming from an older rather dowdy house with no electricity and no running water, Aunt Eileen and Uncle John's amenities seemed majestic.

Uncle John was the Head Librarian of the town—I was very impressed by his title—and the library was located in a separate section of the big house.

After the first day of my "vacation," I knew the sounds that told me cleaning procedures would start and that I could get washed and dressed when they ceased. My impression was of a contented aunt singing as she vacuumed, dusted, and arranged a house that would be perfect for a magazine page, and of a contented wife keeping a shining home and cooking meals for her husband, my Uncle John.

As soon as the vacuum noise ceased, I awaited the sound of singing, assuming this music indicated happiness. In our house, music was used for relaxation, entertainment, and celebration. In my view, my aunt sang the old tunes because of their romantic associations. True, the themes were a little mournful ("When I Grow Too Old to Dream," I'll See you Again," "I Will Always Remember"), but in my view, it seemed that older people tended to sing sad songs.

On the second morning, my visit to the bathroom interrupted her morning ritual; she had made it clear that she did not want me out of bed until the cleaning was finished. However, nature compelled a breaking of the rules. I dashed to the bathroom, glancing down the stairs, anticipating an angry glare or a verbal reproach. Leaving the bathroom, I looked to assure safe return and caught a glimpse of Aunt Eileen's face. I was startled to see tear-streaked cheeks and moist eyes. Catching my alarmed gaze, she said, "Because I'm singing, doesn't mean I'm happy. You don't know what I go through and I'm not going to tell you."

I climbed back into bed and lay there feeling stunned. All my preconceptions had been shattered. The visible signs of comfort around me gave me no hint of sadness. Shining mirrors, well-placed flowers, and a voice raised in song were now mere stage settings which could be cleared away in a moment.

I remained in my room, straightened my bed (as was expected) and waited for the call to breakfast. When the call came, I walked downstairs and greeted my aunt as if a routine day were just beginning. We talked and she outlined her day ahead and a little of my part in it.

In the background, a small radio played. I let the sounds distract and waited for an explanation of her tears. Nothing was said, however, and I knew I had stumbled onto something not yet clear to me.

Uncle John rarely appeared. He ate breakfast in the small kitchen, opened the daily paper, and absorbed himself totally. My aunt, always prepared, it seemed, to be contradicted or punished, at least verbally, kept watch over his toast and refilled his teacup faithfully.

Usually he just folded the paper, stood up and said, "I've got work to do," but on this morning he said "We'll go in to the children's today and get a few books." My aunt always seemed to intervene before my dry mouth could reply. "Say 'Thank you, Uncle John'."

He walked me through to the library to the large, clean newly-installed shelves; the smell of fresh wood filled my senses. Speech totally evaded me; I was in book heaven, never having seen so many volumes in my short life. Uncle John ventured a wintry smile and encouraged me to look around.

"We have a children's section," he offered. "They have *Heidi, Black Beauty,* and *Alice in Wonderland.*" He handed me a red, gold-leafed copy of Lewis Carroll's *Alice.* I was afraid to open it. Who knew where my jam-my fingers had been? When had I washed my hands? My aunt, looking stricken, hung over me like a shadow.

"Maybe you won't open it this time" she whispered. "He's very fussy about new books and he is in charge of all of them." I had already put the book back on the shelf; the frozen look on Uncle John's face did not thaw with a smile. I chose an old copy of *Heidi* instead. My instincts were strong, even at that age. I began to feel unwelcome. But I spent the day happily absorbed in the pages of *Heidi,* and finished it by the end of the day.

The next morning at breakfast, Aunt Eileen said, "Try not to read so fast." Evidently I had stunned Uncle John by finishing *Heidi* in one day. He questioned me about it and couldn't believe I read so fast. Did he not realize there was nothing else to do? After her early-morning vacuuming ritual, my aunt continued to clean all day, scrubbing the floors and polishing the wooden tables. (I never knew why; no one ever saw the inside of the house.) I was too young to go outside alone and still had digestive problems, and Aunt Eileen felt sure I would vomit, or worse, if I strayed far from the house.

These fears were realized when, on helping her make jam the next day (I stirred the raspberries in a large pot), I complained of nausea. Annoyed she said, "Oh, you're always nauseated; go sit in the dining room." "But there's a new rug in there," I said nervously. She insisted, however, upon which I sat numbly pale in the sterile room and vomited on the new rug. Uncle John heard about it at lunch. His cool gaze rested on me and I felt like a butterfly in a case when he said, "Maybe you should just keep her in the lav until she stops being sick."

A few days later, Uncle John and my aunt drove me to see his mother. She and her remaining son lived in a large flat area known for horses; indeed her son raised and raced horses. As soon as I entered the kitchen and saw a tall, gaunt woman, I sensed from whence Uncle John's wry smile emanated. Her face was pale; her dark grey hair was swept back, and an apron covered her all-black dress. She gave me a cold hand and proffered a glass of buttermilk. Even my aunt needed courage to say, "Don't give her milk; she can't drink it." John's mother froze me with a look: "Never met a child who couldn't drink milk; what's wrong with her?"

My aunt said, "She was born in America." Her response struck me as funny, but no one laughed. John's mother gave me a cool look; I had failed some kind of test. I felt ashamed, but lacked the wit or knowledge to redeem myself. The visit lasted an hour. I was not spoken to again.

Sunday — and church — presented another mountain for me to climb. Aunt Eileen and I walked to the church and she told me that, if I felt weak, I should leave the church and wait outside for her; she wouldn't accompany me. My tendency was to reach the Communion part of the Mass and then have an "unexplained weakness" as soon as I received the Host. This Sunday was no exception. As soon as I felt ashen cold fingers in my spine and a lightness in my head, I made the long walk towards the light and air at the big doors at the front of the church. I never thought of using a side exit even though there were many. Outside, I felt better; air and sun revived me and I stumbled to a small stone arbor where you could sit unnoticed. My aunt was embarrassed by my weakness; my uncle apparently felt everyone saw me, and said I should have just slinked quietly to a side exit and be unnoticed. It did not help when he said, "Everyone was looking at you," a sensation I was only too well aware of.

My "vacation" ended that afternoon. Our best friend, a priest from a nearby parish, drove to my aunt's house to take me home. To this day, I can still feel the lift in my heart when I saw the familiar black car. Father Maurice had tea with my aunt as I waited patiently.

The drive home was pure bliss, with long stretches of ribbon-straight road with familiar houses, fields, and landmarks. When I spotted our house, I jumped out to see my two sisters. They greeted me excitedly, but the car got all the attention. Nevertheless, my spirits were up. I was home. I was comforted by the familiar, cheerful sounds provided by the three of us girls — enhanced by the constant sound of the radio and the happy noises we made.

On my "vacation" at Aunt Eileen's and Uncle John's, I had learned to listen for not only the heard melodies, but also for the "unheard" ones.

# peg mangan

She was the third of many barmaids to work in our pub. Peg came from Offaly, a name that meant little to me, but I liked her at once. She was not pretty, but large and well muscled, with a very nice smile.

I was still in the throes of being a sick child, constantly in a state of nausea or having just finished vomiting. Peg walked me through the garden during many of these "sick times" when fresh air and walking seemed to relieve whatever "ailed" me.

Peg talked to me and told me of her childhood in Offaly. She was one of ten children and lived on a farm. Being a girl, she was unable to stay in Offaly—the family could not support her or send her to school. So she answered an ad in the paper and found her way to our pub. The salary was only fair, but she had "bed and board" and Sundays off.

Peg fell foul of my mother early on. My mother had a streak of snobbishness and, more importantly, tended to be jealous where we kids were concerned. My mother did not handle childhood illness well. She hated blood, actually fainted frequently herself, and was nauseated at the sight of vomit or anything worse. Peg was totally unfazed by scrapes, bruises, or vomit. She dealt with it with smiling efficiency.

Most of our workers made good marriages when they had circulated in our pub and grocery. Peg was no exception. Within a year, a young farmer was a fixture in our pub. He was big, handsome, and he persisted. I did not want Peg to leave and tried to discourage the match. Dan was hardworking, gregarious and was smart enough to charm Granny as well as Peg. Within six months they were engaged.

The "Promise of Marriage," as it was then called, did not involve a ring; just a promise of a wedding and talk of dates and "Banns" being called in the church. Romance was difficult. Peg worked hard and Dan did not have time for "the pictures" or an evening out, so courting took place in our "snug" at the back of the pub. We kids tried to stay close to Peg, but were kept under watch in our small living room.

One day as I was sitting at the shop counter in a spot allowed by Granny — out of reach of candy or biscuits and out of sight of any customers who might need privacy — Peg's fiancé came to the counter, his face showing anxiety. I sensed there was something wrong. Dan was never seen before the end of the day. Granny took him into the "snug." I knew I was not wanted. I did not need the stern glance from Granny to hang back, reluctantly. They stayed outside my hearing for a long time. Finally, Granny appeared and, to my astonishment, brought along a fresh bottle of Jameson whiskey and two glasses, not even glancing in my direction.

Supper was delayed; Dan left in an hour look-ing very grim, but, fortified by the Jameson, with some color back in his face. I followed Granny into the kitchen. Peg had appeared to relieve her in the shop.

My mother questioned the delay in supper. "I waited," she complained. Granny replied, "Peg will have a lot of trouble. Dan is being sued for breach of promise."

I was intrigued; what did it mean?, "Breach of promise?" I was told that a former girlfriend of Dan's had been promised a ring and marriage some months ago. Now that Peg was to marry Dan, the former girlfriend had obtained a lawyer and would sue.

I was torn between curiosity, anxiety, and a small feeling of relief. Maybe the marriage would not take place and Peg would stay and take care of me. A heart broken could easily be mended. I was torn.

Poor Peg; how little I knew. Her face was drawn, and for a few days she cried and spent quiet time in her room. We were kept from her, and, in truth , she did not want us near.

The other woman — finally, we heard her name. It was Miss Connolly, our dance teacher. To find that she was the person whose "promise" had been breached left our loyalties somewhat strained. We liked Miss Connolly; she was nice to us and had never hurt us, and Peg was like a family member.

Weeks passed; much talk took place — always in a quiet spot away from us. Poor Peg looked grim and obviously in pain. She stuck with Dan and continued to act as though she would be a bride in a few months. Eventually the case was settled; Dan paid the settlement. No one knew where the money came from. The wedding took place and Peg and Dan left on their honeymoon — a short one as money was by now quite scarce. We gave up the dance lessons when Miss Connolly moved out of the area, never to be heard from again.

Peg and Dan moved back onto a farm some miles from our village. Reports came back that Peg was a tireless worker, kept the house clean, and was a great asset on the farm. An admirer proclaimed in our pub, "She's as good as any young lad I ever saw; work is no trouble to her."

Unfortunately, Peg did not live long on the farm she apparently loved. She died at the age of forty-four. Dan stayed on the farm and remarried a year later. He eventually had several strong sons to help him.

# Brilliant Family

In our small village, it was common to know all the families—and their eccentricities. The Misses McHugh lived in a small dark house surrounded by trees, and when we heard the loud barking of their dogs, we imagined them to be huge animals ready to eat small children. The Misses McHugh were well known in the area, although not often seen.

Stories of the "brilliant" McHughs were oft related. As we grew more curious, we learned that they spoke French, read novels, and played music at home. Miss Julia played the organ in church. She played loudly but off key, and as the choir was always off key, we knew not whom to blame. Miss Maddy (short for Madeline, but we kids thought it meant her mental status) wrote pious stories for religious magazines (some of which were familiar to us as Granny read them aloud, perhaps hoping to get us to emulate the saints described in them). Miss Molly was obese, very pleasant, and seemed content to shop and cook, and feed the dogs.

One evening when I was a curious ten-year-old, one of their two brothers, Denis McHugh, appeared in our pub. (I was sometimes forgotten as an observer, but

I carefully watched and listened when I could.) He was a small man whose glasses sat low on his nose; he dressed in a long grey coat, a scarf floating across his throat. He looked like a Victorian dandy I had seen in a magazine.

Soon Doctor Denis revealed talents other than medical training. He frequented our pub, sitting in the "snug," where he drank glasses of whiskey and talked to anyone who would listen. Granny and the barmaid were too busy to pay attention, so one or all of us would sit in and listen until boredom set in.

His stories were of medicine and training and his experience in the world and how much he hated his three sisters, whom he described as "the three witches." He claimed that they watered his whiskey and had trained the dogs to bark when he left the house for our bar. His description of their house enthralled me; he told how the sisters kept the oil lamps low and used smoky glass as shades so that he could not read. It sounded medieval and possibly untrue, but I had developed an affection for this strange man and believed all his tales.

He often talked to us three girls about our health. He obsessed about our teeth and he was appalled at our ignorance of what he called "the facts of life." We had a vague belief that babies came from cabbages. We also believed in Santa, fairies, and "the little people," as we had been told. Doctor Denis did not reveal sexual secrets, but once, at a late stage of drinking, spoke of "wedded bliss" and the need for women to care for their men and avoid annoying them.

As his drinking problem increased, and mental confusion set in, his appearance deteriorated to the point where he appeared in the pub in his pajamas covered by his heavy coat. Granny would put him into the "snug," out of sight of customers. He was now traveling home by hired car from the pub, as walking was too difficult for him.

Months slipped by and we kids lost interest in Doctor Denis and his problems. I sometimes spotted him as I dashed past the "snug." He would sit, shrouded in smoke from the fire, whiskey glass on the table, singing snatches of songs, and, on occasion, reciting bits of poetry.

Unexpectedly, one day we heard that Doctor Denis had fallen into a well at the back of his sisters' house and drowned. Apparently, he wandered out in the night looking for the outhouse and fell into the well, the cover of which had been removed and inadvertently not replaced. Doctor Denis had died in the dark without friend or family. We prayed that his alcoholic haze had saved him from panic or pain.

# Billy Huck

The bar area in our pub/grocery was "off lim-its" to all children, and as I wandered in and out of the shop, I learned to avoid it. But on unguarded days, I could walk past the bar to the door behind it which led to the private part of the house, and I became aware of certain familiar figures at the bar.

On one of these occasions, I observed a sad-faced, red-headed man who had no teeth and was in poor shape. He spoke very nicely to me and said he was Billy Huck. He proffered a grimy hand and made a vague effort to remove his battered cap, already pushed to the back of his head. I took the hand and then quickly made my way through the back door, knowing sharp ears would have heard my voice.

During the years that followed, I grew to know Billy fairly well. He was the only son of a local woman and she had poured much of her life savings into his education. Billy Huck, unlike most of his schoolmates, had actually gone to a local college. He had been an altar boy and one time had thought of being a priest. But somewhere along the way, Billy "fell among thieves," to use Granny's expression. He quit college, began to drink, and, by the time I met him, he barely managed a day on the farm without a pint or two of stout.

Inside, he was a quiet, somewhat depressed man given to bemoaning his state and trying to recall his days of learning. As soon as he drank, his speech became garbled; half sentences of Spanish, Latin, and pieces of poetry came from him. He could easily become maudlin, but usually was asked to vacate the premises before he reached that state.

Billy survived meagerly on his small farm. His mother tried to keep money away from him, but he learned to steal fresh eggs laid by their hens and sell them in the village for beer. When his mother died, late in her eighties, Billy discovered a small amount of cash hidden in the mattress of her bed. It provided a decent burial for her and gave him enough to go on a long bender to mourn her passing.

Shortly afterward, Billy took "the pledge," swearing to abstain from all drink for a year, and began to talk of marriage. To the astonishment of all the neighbors, he married and settled into quiet respectability, and his wife bore several children.

After he married, I saw Billy once or twice in the village or at Mass, his red hair always the identifying sign. But eventually Billy's sobriety suffered a mortal blow — celebrating his son's confirmation, he fell off the wagon and began to descend into a vortex of booze.

As the years slipped by, Billy deteriorated into a semi-conscious condition. He drank early, and by evening was asleep outside the pub — any pub — that would still serve him. His children grew into the habit of picking him up and ferrying him home — in their early years, on a bicycle, and then later on in an old, battered, red truck. Billy would protest feebly, then lapse into song or garbled poetry. Billy died quietly in his bed in the small cottage he inherited from his mother. Five red-haired sons saw him off.

middle years

# swimming with swans

he drawing room of our house had been off limits to us as small children. As three noisy girls, we tended to "wreck every room in the house" (my mother's phrase). But as we grew older, the room became available to us on special occasions. On Sundays it became a venue for lessons in waltzing and social behavior, and for the teaching of "party pieces" for our debuts into "society." At this time, however, "society" seemed to us as remote as Australia — in our small Irish village, Sunday Mass and the Mission Mass once a month were the height of excitement.

Learning to waltz, sing ballads, and make conversation seemed to us to be like teaching swans to fly where there was no water around or a likelihood of rain. However, we wanted to please our mother — the pianist and social arbiter of our group. We patiently learned to waltz (with much stepping on toes), then walked with books on our heads to give us a "straight carriage" and "elegant bearing."

Singing proved a slow painful lesson for two of us. Our sister of the curly hair, Patricia, had a lovely voice and was keen on singing. As the youngest, I had a weak voice and a very shy disposition. My older sister, Mona (the rebel), resisted every event suggested by the family. Time began to provide patterns for the drawing room classes, and eventually we had fun. We began to enjoy singing and even dancing together. Granny joined the entertainments on Sundays (when the pub was closed), and her wit and talent infected us.

As we grew into our mid teens, a few select young men were included in the group. They were in their twenties, of respectable background, and real friends of the family. We were encouraged to dance with them and listen to stories of their social experience. Living as we did in an all-female household, the presence of men of *whatever* age or state was a whole new experience which both fascinated and puzzled us. The Sunday evening sessions continued, with an occasional sense of a real "party" in progress.

One day, a local wealthy banker, who lived just outside of town, stopped into Granny's pub for a drink. Sensing an opportunity for us three girls, Granny bragged to him about our "considerable" talents. She hoped that if we could make a good impression, this wealthy man might offer us jobs one day — or might know someone who had openings. And, even by this time, we three girls, like our mother, had started dreaming of future lives far from the village.

Granny was convincing, and the wealthy banker invited us to dinner at his beautiful house nearby just outside the village. A Rolls Royce collected us on a few Sundays. Arriving wide-eyed at the house, we thought it looked like Tara in *Gone with the Wind.* We were expected to enjoy dinner, to use the right cutlery, drink a little wine, and sing and be entertaining.

We were in "society" and briefly popular. But even in our inexperienced lives, we could appreciate that we were a novelty — we were there to provide music and some funny "stories" to keep after-dinner guests amused.

We girls drank dry sherry in small glasses that we were unaccustomed to. The sherry and a huge coal fire gave us a flushed look and we lost any shyness when dinner ended and we moved to the piano. As usual, my mother played. Rarely relieved of this duty, she had alerted us to refill her glass whenever it was empty.

The meal ended with brandy and coffee, and even cigars (outside the drawing room) for the men. The ambience was, to us, exotic, totally new, and very enticing. We performed well and were driven home in the gleaming Rolls Royce.

Granny wanted to hear every detail of both the menu and the entertainment. We always replayed our triumph — emphasizing and exaggerating any compliments received.

These evenings continued here and there throughout our teens, but came to an end when our host suffered a stroke and the "grand" house was eventually sold.

How much we learned from our drawing room "swimming" lessons is hard to evaluate. Perhaps we learned to be social, how to handle unusual situations, how to deal with different social occasions. We weren't offered jobs — as Granny had hoped — but we were comfortable with whatever society presented.

It was Cinderella-like for a few brief years. Our coach finally disappeared and Prince Charming never showed — at least not in the drawing room, and never on a lake with swans.

# collette

ne day when we were in our early teens, a young woman came into our pub—her appearance and style markedly different from the usual staid customers. Her name was Collette–even the name (not a saint's name as was the custom) suggested an exotic mystery. We found her make-up (red lipstick and red nails) quite shocking and thrilling–a sign for sure, we thought, of hidden scandal and intrigue.

We had long heard about Collette from village gossip. She had grown up near the village—a sheltered, repressed, and spoiled only child of older parents. She had never been taught to help with the house, and spent time dreaming and reading romance novels. Following a standard education at the local elementary school, she had learned sewing, deportment, and a little French from the Belgian nuns who ran a school for young girls. (These nuns had arrived as refugees at the beginning of the war, and no one knew how they had chosen our small village in the south of Ireland.) She had grown into an overweight young woman, with thick glasses and a blotchy complexion—very shy and gauche.

When Colette was in her thirties, her mother died suddenly. Collette was relieved to finally be free, and she found herself suddenly quite wealthy as well—her family owned land and had invested wisely. Without her mother's repression, she changed her appearance totally. She lost weight, wore fashionable glasses and adopted heavy make-up—with red lipstick (a sign of decadence to villagers). She often wore red hats and high heels (not a common sight at that time and considered impractical in our rough terrain), and she caused quite a stir with her appearance at Mass.

She also took driving lessons, a rare sight in an area where women let their husbands drive, or secretly took lessons on the roads at night, where no one would witness their mistakes. She bought a shiny new car, and drove all through the roads, smoking and waving or honking at passers-by on foot.

She relished a new-found taste for sherry, preferring a "dry" sherry and asking to see the label when she visited a pub (in her case a few pubs). Within a year, her presence at the bar in the local hotel was a familiar, if daunting, sight. The locals (mostly men) were shocked speechless to see a woman sitting so comfortably at the bar—and smoking through a long cigarette holder.

So when Collette walked into our pub, we were surprised and intrigued and didn't know what to expect. But when we had all recovered from the shock of her make-up and dress, and got into lengthy conversations with her, we found Collette to be a very generous and educated woman just glad to "get away from a dull life with older parents." My mother was fascinated by her and soon Collette was invited into our small living room–away from the noise of the bar. My sisters and I formed an immediate bond and deepening friendship with Collette, and gradually she introduced us to life away from our small village.

As we grew older, she took us girls on trips up to Dublin, and we were allowed to spend a few days in the hotel away from our usual surroundings. Away from home in a busy city, we were excited and intrigued by the traffic and noise. We saw movies late at night—a treat to be enjoyed past our normal bedtime. Collette introduced us to theater, bookstores, museums, and local spots hitherto unheard of and generally for adults—another treat. None of these experiences were even faintly wicked or scandalous, but being away from our mother's restrictions and our dull routine was to us a joyous get-away.

Our new friend gave us advice on growing up and correct behavior in company, and often bought us fashionable clothing, which we loved, but could not afford.

Inevitably, my mother grew jealous and suspicious–her daughters were away from her control and a threat to the well-ordered life she had planned for us all. She restricted, and eventually cancelled, the trips away, and Collette gradually faded out of our lives. But we treasured those experiences and her lessons, and they prepared us for our lives ahead in more ways than we could know then.

Years passed before I encountered Collette again. The occasion was to celebrate her surprising engagement at her "advanced" age of 44. But the marriage didn't last long and was shrouded in intrigue. Collette's harrowing experience held yet another lesson which we would soon learn.

# "commitments" and secrets

It was a shocking event that caused Collette to question and re-evaluate her new marriage—she awoke one morning to find her husband sitting with a loaded shotgun at her bedside.

She had married a well-known local farmer. They were both over 40 and the locals felt it was "time" for the two of them to marry. Her parish priest encouraged the pair, and performed the ceremony, giving one of his long sermons extolling the virtues of a state he was totally ignorant of. Father Duneen gave the groom a wonderful endorsement, praising his steady loyalty to the church, and to his aging parents.

Collette's marriage to Patrick seemed to be a good idea to her. She liked having an escort, being taken to dinner in Dublin, and having a man take care of things. Patrick seemed quiet but, at times, funny. He was amused by her dress and makeup, and enjoyed the stir she created—a woman, smoking with a long holder, sipping sherry, and blissfully unaware of the talk around her.

The first few months of their marriage were quiet. He walked the land, now partly his, and noted all the labor ahead of him when the weather allowed; she sat in her robe and read all day and listened to the radio.

Their first trouble came about when he asked her to prepare a meal for the workers who had labored all day in the fields. He strongly suggested she rise early to allow time to prepare a good meal. Reluctantly she agreed, but allowing herself the luxury of keeping her bathrobe on and taking a long toilette, she had even less, not more, time to prepare.

Arriving home with his crew, Patrick found that Colette had prepared cucumber sandwiches, thinly sliced, and fit for afternoon tea. Her big surprise was an apple pie covered with whipped cream. She had added the color purple to the confection, feeling this would cheer the men. Their first row occurred after this incident. Patrick had been humiliated seeing the workers titter and give pitying looks in his direction. Colette sulked for a day, staying in their room, until he forgave her.

As the months progressed, she became aware of a change in Patrick's manner. Formerly serene, he began to behave sullenly, not speaking, walking for long periods, missing meals, and refusing to speak when he returned. Her efforts to amuse or annoy him were rejected. He often sat in their large living room for hours, staring into space.

When Colette awoke one morning to his appearance at her bedside with the gun, she felt cold fear and was speechless for a full minute. "I was going to shoot you." His voice was flat. And he added simply, "Then I would have shot myself. Maybe I should be committed again."

Rage overcame her, and a mounting resentment began to well up. She needed advice and decided

to seek the help of the parish priest. She drove slowly to his house but her thoughts were  racing ahead.

Father Duneen greeted her calmly, if a little absently,
and she poured out her tale to him. He listened without
comment, and paused for a long time after listening to her
tale. "You have to take better care of your spouse," he stated
firmly. "Patrick is a fine man. You must have upset him."

"Did you know his mental state when you married us?" Colette felt the anger in her tone and tried to
control herself, though tears of rage were forming. Fr.
Duneen clasped his frail hands in what seemed to resem-
ble a prayerful mode. "Now my dear Collette, we have to
keep *some* secrets from you women. Marriage is about find-
ing the good and bad and some weakness in one another.
Patrick had to spend a good few months in the county
asylum. No one knew but myself and his parents." His
voice became soothing—"we didn't want to upset you."

Driving home, she thought how she could proceed.
Being Catholic, divorce was not an option; it seemed a separation was her only choice. But she had signed papers
when they became engaged, and having had a few drinks
before the signing, she was not too clear as to the content.
Reading the small print when she studied the words at
home, she saw that their property was divided equally
between them, but in the event of "incapacitation" of one
of the pair, his or her family (in this case Patrick's parents)
would take over the entire property. Foolishly, she had
signed—and it seemed, sealed—her future. Talking to Fr.

Duneen had revealed nothing of use for her problems; she was equally sure her in-laws would not be of any help.

Several weeks passed; her husband continued to brood and walk mostly by himself on the land, and he did not speak to her. At times, she felt his gaze on her — a gaze both remote and threatening. Her problem would have been unsolved, but fate intervened. Patrick was killed in a tractor accident one day in the late fall.

His funeral was well attended. Most of the local farmers in the area were there. Colette was carefully observed by those who were aware of her earlier flamboyant attire. On this occasion, however, she wore appropriate garb — black, with suitably subdued accessories, and a mournful look, entirely appropriate to the occasion. But as she was driven away, few of the mourners saw her quiet smile of relief — and the long cigarette holder in her hand.

Secrets, indeed . . .

# final note

My mother insisted that we three girls should enter a "boarding school" run by nuns as soon as we reached our teens. Her thinking was that the nuns might make ladies of us, and she also felt that the local women and their children were not "fit" to mix with us. And, since the school was fairly close to the village, we could easily come home for vacations—and our mother could still keep an eye on us.

I was entered into this culture at the tender age of fifteen, my two older sisters having preceded me—their tuition somehow scraped together by Granny and my mother from the meager pub and grocery income. For me, the opportunity arose sooner than planned as I had the luck to win a small share in a lottery, which helped to pay for one term at school.

On my admission to the convent of St. Luke, about ten miles outside the village, I was at first thrilled to be reunited with my older siblings. My pleasure was dimmed when I was informed that my mother had signed me up for piano lessons. Although I loved hearing it played, I had displayed no aptitude for the instrument. My mother was not to be reasoned with, so I resigned myself to my first lesson.

Sister Lazarius was to be my teacher. She sent a note giving me the directions to her music room in the convent. Arriving at the room, I was struck by its cool, damp, airless feel which only added to my anxiety at meeting my new instructor.

Sister Lazarius was a tall, pale nun dressed in the all-black habit of the order, with a small strip of white at her collar. Her almost colorless face was set off by very blue eyes which should have formed a pleasing contrast to her pallor, but the eyes looking at me were cold and without either softness or expression.

She seated me at the piano and led me in the scales, pointing out the names of the black and white keys, and leaving me with an exercise to practice for our next meeting.

Our lessons proceeded for the next three or four weeks. She sat quietly, and I struggled to match her accuracy. My practice had been spotty, and by now I was sure of my total lack of talent. My fear of those cold blue eyes was great.

Sister Lazarius was not a patient teacher; she did not tolerate mistakes, even at the very first lesson. I was not prepared for her use of a ruler on my inaccurate fingers. The ruler had a steel tip which gave my hands blue marks and would have started tears but for a stubborn reaction on my part to not allow them (at least in the chill of the piano room).

I realized that there were other pupils suffering as I was, and there was no one to complain to — nuns did not correct one another; they stuck together in solidarity. Appealing to my mother would have been effective, but I knew too well that her reaction would be swift and difficult to control. I envisioned her storming into school and demanding an audience with Reverend Mother — a remote figure unseen by students and the leader of the convent and monitor of teaching skills. I imagined my mother staging a scene. The result would surely be reported to all the school, and I might become a figure of ridicule and cowardice for having my mother fight my battle.

Gradually the fear of piano lessons began to affect my daily schoolwork. I began to dread the day before a lesson and felt drained and resentful following the experience.

One night, awake and dreading the next day, I decided to rescue myself. The next morning I slipped away from class. I had written a simple note, and hurried towards the now infamous piano room. My heart thudded and my palms felt sweaty — I was out of bounds and could be in trouble if found away from class and in the nuns' area, and not for an approved reason. Luckily, the corridor was empty and I crept forward, finally reaching the room. I laid the note on the piano cover. I felt proud of my note. It said, simply, "Dear Sister Lazarius, I have given up the piano." I had signed my name (clearly, if not steadily) at the bottom. I flew back to class on wings. I was free. No one knew what I had done, and I had not had coaching from a soul.

That evening at supper, I was flushed and the Sister in charge of the dining room sent me to the infirmary to be seen by the "nurse." I set out lightheartedly. I reached the dormitory where the Sister nurse was to see me. I was stunned to see that Sister Lazarius was the assigned nurse.

As I sat on a small white-covered cot, a new sensation washed over me — how would my former piano teacher treat me? I sat still, not breathing, as she took my temperature and felt for glands in my neck. She made no comment, but said I could get ready for bed. "I will have supper sent over," she stated flatly, "and I will get you some aspirin and hot milk." Her manner was cool, professional, and above reproach. I changed into my bathrobe to offset the chill of the dormitory and awaited the arrival of my evening meal—always cold, and not improved by the long trip from the dining room some distance away.

Oddly triumphant, I now had a story to tell my friends—I had faced my demon and had survived, to my own surprise. My mother accepted defeat, and I had enough sense to mute my criticism of my teacher, explaining my departure from the music scene as being due to a lack of talent. This incident remained clearly etched in my mind, perhaps because it represented my first challenge to authority—decisive action had not previously been one of my strong points.

# soᴨg foᴚ sisteᴚ `a`

**D**uring my first week in our boarding school, I was informed about the "new girls' concert"that would be held at the end of the month. The custom was to "break in" newcomers to relieve shyness and to allow the nuns to watch for new talent, as the tradition was to stage operettas as a cultural lesson for the girls in school. Though very shy, I was not fazed by the challenge. Growing up, I had learned that everyone had to develop a talent for performing in any gathering at home or elsewhere. No one was excused, regardless of shyness, age, disposition, or talent—or lack thereof.

I knew I could sing and had a sweet voice, and also assumed that the girls might accept me more readily if I gave my best at the concert, even if they felt my skills were meager. On the "big night" of the concert, I felt my heart pounding. My throat was dry and I was flushed. As I stepped forward, I awaited the opening notes of the pianist and let my eyes screen the audience. There they sat, rows of nuns in black and white, like attentive penguins.

Behind them, a few rows away — and looking as new as I felt — were the novices, all in white and with expressions of anxiety, showing that they, too, had just started a new life.

I heard the opening note and started to sing. My choice of song was "The Spinning Wheel," a popular ballad of the time, often heard on the radio. As I finished the first verse, the pianist began to play again, indicating that a second verse would be acceptable. My eyes began to scan the audience; now I was calm enough to see faces. As my gaze swept the last row, I saw that one of the novices, all in white, had tears running down her face. My first reaction was one of astonishment, then of anxiety. What was the cause of the tears?

This was my first experience with nuns; they were a new breed to me. They appeared to dwell on a higher plane than ordinary people, and this created a sense of awe in me. All the teaching nuns wore a black habit with a large, white, bib-like collar; they seemed to glide along the corridors without a sound and had the ability to see an infraction of a rule with one glance. All the faces were tightly bound by the headdress and it was impossible to tell age or health or sometimes emotion.

I hurried off stage; a few girls awaited me with new interest. They had all seen the tears on the face of the young nun and asked, "Why did she cry?" A few had a romantic idea of the cause — one theory was a broken love affair with the song as a reminder. Other girls (of the Romeo and Juliet school) felt that the romance had ended tragically. I was famous, just for a moment and not for my singing, but for the effect I caused — getting a nun to cry, and in public, was a feat.

Weeks went by and I was no longer "famous." I was settling into the routine when I saw the novice (the one who cried) in the chapel, praying. I decided to wait outside. Surely the novice would see me and tell me the story of her tears. But the young nun hurried past me, unaware of my presence, and entered the convent. I was tempted to ring the bell and ask her about her tears, but decided not to. The novice could keep her secret, if there was one. If a song recalled a memory of her past, it was hers to keep. She was on a new path; her life would continue, just as mine would.

# silver wings away

My sister Mona was seventeen when she fell in love, or at least was seventeen when a suitor called on her. He was part of a big family who lived nearby; there were eight boys and two girls. He had joined the Royal Air Force and had come home on leave. In his uniform, he created a stir in our small village. He had beautiful manners and was extremely polite, a trait not yet visible in his kin.

We did not witness the beginning of the blossoming romance. Perhaps they met out walking, but more likely our hero had a drink at our pub while Mona was there. His name was Michael and he asked to make a visit to meet my mother and, we hoped to "ask for Mona's hand."

As the younger sisters, we had no idea what that meant, but we saw an opportunity here. We had had many gripes with Mona throughout our growing years. She got to stay up later and she had the first wearing of clothes. We inherited them only after she had worn them past all our visions of fashion. If she married (although unlikely at that early age), we would have a wedding and a chance to wear new dresses. *Any* groom would have been welcome.

Michael was deferential to my mother and brought her a bottle of Evening in Paris, her favorite perfume. We listened avidly to the conversation. Michael did not offer to take Mona away, but asked if he could visit the house and perhaps take her to the pictures.

My mother felt that the evening would be prolonged conversation-wise to no effect, so she decided to bring a gramophone to the kitchen and play a record for entertainment. Since there was only one couple present who could dance, Michael and Mona, seemingly not embarrassed by this strange set-up, moved slowly around the kitchen in a fox-trot. We sat on the kitchen steps. My mother moved around the table, sat down and tried not to appear as if she were watching the couple — which was precisely why she was there.

Michael had brought a Vera Lynn record for my sister; Vera was very popular during the war. Her "We'll Meet Again" song was on BBC daily. To my disappointment, the record he brought was "Silver Wings in the Moonlight," hitherto unknown to us. The lyrics spoke of a plane flying during the war and asking the plane to take care of the pilot. We listened to the lyrics with some disappointment. It was unfamiliar, and we preferred the familiar song.

As the couple moved slowly around the floor, however, I began to relieve my boredom by listening closely to the lyrics. There was a possibility that Mona's suitor might be flying in the war; might even be killed. I had admired the uniform, but was too young to think of the future he faced. Flying was unknown to me. I had never seen a plane and was too young, my mother thought, for war movies.

As the song continued and we rewound the gramophone, the lyrics touched a vague chord. "Keep him safely and then, silver wings in the moonlight, bring him homeward again." My vivid imagination sketched a picture of death in the air and my sister, a beautiful young Irish widow, living in London with lots of room for her two sisters to visit. Life would be hard, but shrouded in romance, clouds, drama, people talking to us, and, more importantly, *about* us.

The evening ended. Michael and Mona said goodbye surrounded by all of us. In the decidedly unromantic venue, they just swore to write to one another.

Michael promised a diamond ring in a few months and my mother received a kiss on the cheek — something which she rarely allowed, but suffered politely.

The end was uneventful. A few weeks after Michael's departure, Mona met the handsome son of a local station agent and began to see him. Michael's letters faded, and soon his name was not mentioned in the house. "Silver Wings" is probably unknown, and I have never heard it sung again.

# Later years

# Destination USA

One of Granny's favorite pronouncements to us girls through the years was, "You will all go to America when you grow up. You will meet your father."

Our mother's life-long ambition, however, was to move with us and Granny to Dublin. But that dream never materialized. When my mother left the village, it was to London—without Granny and with only two of us girls close by, but never all of us together.

After boarding school, my sisters and I had all begun to travel to England to pursue careers. Mona and Patricia each entered different fields and eventually settled in England, and I entered nursing training and then worked in England for a few years, too. We had all left the village in search of new venues and new experiences, but gradually, and separately, we would all return to America—initially, each for a different reason, but all with the aim of someday meeting our father back in Brooklyn.

When I was 29, a friend suggested I apply for a job on a cruise ship. I had no idea what a "cruise" meant, and even less about my possible role there, but in an interview with the shipowner, he mentioned that follow-

101

ing the "shakedown cruise," the new liner would sail for America. My future became fixed; I signed on and awaited the day when we would land in New York.

On the cruise to New York, I was filled with both excitement and trepidation. Who was this man listed as "Father" on my birth certificate? In my teens I had begun to form a picture of him, resorting to the male movie stars I saw in films in Ireland in the 1940s. At first, Robert Young seemed a likely, comfortable "Dad" image. Later Spencer Tracy seemed a more realistic model. Then Pat O'Brien became my ideal "Dad" working in New York and living in Brooklyn, my birthplace. Finally, I decided he would be a combination of them all.

But those blissful images in my mind were tempered by the harsh ones my mother had so bitterly painted for us growing up. Would I meet a Pat O'Brien/Robert Young/Spencer Tracy "Dad" or a womanizing, philandering deadbeat?

My ship finally docked in New York and Mona met me at the landing; she had preceded me to America and had already met our father. Her expectations had been high—perhaps too high—and evidently things had not gone well. Unfortunately, their reunion had ended in disappointment.

But, plans were already in place for *my* "family reunion." A friend of my father's (a young man who had grown up in Brooklyn and whose mother was the Irish connection with my father) had arranged for a meeting in New York. The friend was excited and intrigued at the thought of a reunion in his apartment. The day of reckoning had finally come.

# "not spencer tracy"

I was torn between excitement and fear, blending with shyness. I was about to have a reunion with a father I had never met, in a strange house, being observed by a young man I had only met once.

Waiting for the doorbell to ring, I calmed and distracted myself by deep breathing, studying the furniture in the room, and listening to unending traffic noises.

The doorbell finally rang at 2 o'clock and, in a moment, a knock signaled the arrival of the stranger I was about to meet. The man who came into view was small, neatly dressed, and had a ruddy complexion and blue eyes. His expression mirrored mine–anxiety, shyness, and a slightly guarded look. We had barely communicated over the years and had only our bloodline in common.

I had heard my mother's version of what had happened so long ago, but never my father's. It was clear that he was a very pleasant, guarded man, with an accent as strong as when he left his native Mayo so long ago.

We shook hands and our cheeks touched very briefly. He sat across from me and accepted a glass of water from Martin, our host. Martin initiated some small talk and I joined in — noting the cool weather, New York's unending traffic, and my shipboard travels to the Caribbean.

My father's eyes rarely left my face, and I saw instantly how a casual comment from me would send a faint smile or a stern look in my direction.

I waited to tell him how my mother — his wife — was and to update him about the remaining daughter he had yet to meet. I knew that he had already met Mona, but when I mentioned her name, I gathered from the look on his face he didn't want to talk about her. They were currently "not on good terms," he said simply.

I then introduced one or two small topics relating to school, life with nuns, boarding school, and some of Granny's pithy comments. The room lightened–or at least the mood seemed to — when I referenced the past.

By now I was somewhat relaxed–still watching my father's blue eyes and observing any mood changes on his rather guarded face. I had started calling him "Pop" — which seemed to please him. Other titles seemed inappropriate: "Daddy" was too young and "Father" reminded me of the clergy back in our village. So my choice brought the first real warmth to his face.

My clothing met with quiet approval. Pop did not like pants on women. My skirt and heavy sweater were warm and apparently non-threatening. Mona, on the other hand liked hats and (he felt) wore too much make-up and smoked constantly. I had not been able to acquire a cigarette habit and had passed out with my first martini. So I felt a breath of relief–I was almost perfect, so far.

And so our meeting continued, easing slowly forward, but more and more comfortably. I wanted to know what had happened those many years ago that landed us in Ireland without him. But I sensed a reluctance on Pop's part to talk about the past, at least in any detail. He revealed only bits and pieces of his side of the story, but when he told me that he still had Mona's little red tricycle, I knew that "Father," "Dad," "Pop," or even "him" as described angrily by my mother was not a gangster, wife-beater, or aging lothario as her past references had depicted. The man who was not a movie star or mogul was a sensitive, wounded, and isolated being who had suffered great sadness.

As the time approached for farewell (Pop wanted to catch an early subway), I felt relief, affection, and sympathy for this new addition to my life. We parted quickly — cheeks touching again. The hand on my shoulder tightened slightly — almost a hug — a step begun on a long road leading to a reality far from the movie set I had envisioned. *His* past now became an important, long-lost part of *my* past.

# "home soon"

As far as my father, Andrew, had been concerned, his wife, Elizabeth, was going back to her mother's in Ireland for a visit. The trip would be long and arduous; boarding a ship with three small children, the youngest barely a year old, would be a challenge. His wife assured him that after a vacation and a little rest in Ireland, they would all come back. Their part of Brooklyn in 1930 was full of Irish, Italian, and Polish families. They shared stories on the block. She had learned from the other women that pregnancy would be her lot for the next few years; already she was worn out; her first born had cried constantly for the first six months.

My father had not been sure how to handle this imminent separation. He tried to reconcile himself to the upcoming departure but found himself unable to grasp its significance. Elizabeth, quietly but relentlessly, continued to talk of the trip, even shopped for clothes and spoke of the change in climate. Ireland did not have long, humid summers she reminded him. Food would be different; the three small children would be living in a farming village.

He knew well the surroundings that would be facing the kids; he had lived there himself. Why did she speak as if all this stuff were strange to him? He knew about fat bacon, green cabbage, potatoes, brown bread, and strong milk, not in bottles but fresh from the cows. He imagined the kids, small curious creatures, living on a big ship for many days. They would land in Cobh, Cork, then be driven the long journey home. How would they adjust? Would they miss him?

Days hurried by and he felt the upcoming parting looming larger every morning. He had avoided talk of the trip feeling that if he did not speak of it, she might have a change in plans. She was tired; he knew the heat exhausted her; her skin and hair were too fair for this climate. Always a poor eater, she ate only dried biscuits in the summer heat. For their part, the children were healthy as far as he could tell.

Finally, the weekend before the departure had arrived; they would sail on Wednesday. Suitcases were appearing in the small kitchen, and he saw a passport with the two small faces and one picture of Elizabeth with the baby in her arms. She looked sad and unsmiling in the picture, but, surely, seeing Ireland again and visiting her mother would restore her to health and vitality. He reasoned that marriage at an early age, money problems, and three pregnancies in three years was a heavy burden for a young girl.

The day arrived; it was a very early departure. He called a taxi, loaded luggage, and helped with the kids. They were quiet, sleepy, and mildly excited. The baby cried all the way to the dock, apparently from the noise and clatter.

He didn't delay good-byes. Later he realized that he had not kissed Elizabeth once, just tried to hold the girls for a long moment, murmuring he knew not what until someone called out and they were hurried away. He went home by subway, unaware of stops and people; a slow dullness seemed to have numbed him.

Entering the apartment, he had the feeling of dread. An emptiness he expected, but this was a new feeling. He would be alone for the next few months, and time would drag; but he would survive. He could count the days on the calendar in the kitchen. It would help to focus him, he thought; but he did not know for how long. He — and we — could not have foreseen that the wait would be 29 years.

# old hat

As the years passed after our reunion in Brooklyn, I saw my father often, and later my sister Patricia came to America and met him as well. When Patricia became engaged, our mother back in London wrote to say that she would attend the wedding, having missed both Mona's and mine.

The wedding reception was to be held in my newly acquired home in New Jersey on a lovely autumn day in the early seventies. My husband and I were thrilled to host a small gathering, but my feelings and that of the bride's focused on the reality that for the first time we would see our parents together in one place.

Wedding preparations went on smoothly; it had been planned for a small group of friends well known to all of us. My sister and I shopped for her wedding dress, and my bridesmaid's outfit. As we shopped, we spoke of the upcoming reunion of our parents and how it would develop.

Our view of two long-separated people was by now somewhat colored by fantasy — growing up we had always hoped that our father would look like Robert Young or Spencer Tracy. Our mother had matured into a striking, slim, silver blond woman with good taste and grooming, and we saw her as Greer Garson in our "film re-enactment" of the meeting.

Romance was all around us; my husband and I were broke but happy in our ten-year marriage, and the bride, Patricia, although more mature, radiated bliss. This may explain our misty-eyed illusion of the great reunion of the two people who had brought us into this world so long ago.

We wondered if the setting of their meeting should be made more private. Should the couple, parted forty years earlier, be left alone in one of the small rooms off the porch? Frankly, this idea did not fit our plans, since we wished to be onlookers and witnesses to a great romantic scene; traces of old movies intruded on reality. We rather hoped to acquire a new set of parents who would give their blessing to the bride of the day and to one of the married daughters present. We envisioned joy and blessings and smiles from the two people we had reunited.

The wedding went off nicely. My parents were there, separated in different seats — we had thought a meeting in the church might be inappropriate. My mother planned to join the reception a little late ("making an entrance," we called it); so we drove Pop to the house and made him a stiff drink.

Guests mingled downstairs where drinks and food were available. My mother arrived, and I ran to the door to give her time to check her makeup and hair, ready for her big scene. She looked lovely — hair shining, borrowed pearls — and seemed relaxed. My father came to the door of the room and I stood between them — my eyes and attention divided between two people I knew well and, it seemed, not at all.

Pop spoke clearly two words which did not adhere to our fantasy script. "What's new?," he said calmly. I turned to my mother, awaiting her answer. She said, "You're still wearing that stupid old hat."

The new bride and I felt as if the lights had been dimmed and the hidden orchestra slipped away unheard. So much for Spencer Tracy and Greer Garson . . . But evidently, for our parents, years and an ocean apart may have dulled, but hadn't extinguished, their feelings for each other. They subsequently became friends, if a little guardedly at first, but with no anger or recriminations.

My mother decided to stay in New York (in Manhattan), and in their remaining years our mother and father became telephone friends on a weekly basis.

For a few months at first, homesickness had enveloped my mother—even missing the small village and narrow people she had always abhorred. In her later years, she did reunite with her sisters back in Ireland, making each return home a celebration, filling the parties with tales of fashions and lifestyles of New York.

My mother had always prayed for a sudden death, wanting to be "no trouble to anyone."Her prayers were answered, and she died peacefully in her small apartment. My father died less than two weeks later.

Both had left a request for cremation and no fuss or ceremony. Their ashes were flown to Ireland and were interred in the village where we grew up—and which my mother had never really left behind after all.

# epilogue

Our beloved Granny, back in Ballylin, had become ill and increasingly frail in the many years after we had all left the village. Eventually the pub and shop were sold and she moved in with her sisters. Sadly, Granny died while I was on the ship on my way to America to meet my father.

When she died, no priest came to meet the hearse on its long journey from Dublin to the village graveyard in Ballylin. My aunt, furious and alone at the funeral procession, called the parish and said, "This woman gave priests breakfasts for years; someone should come down to bury her." Finally someone did—a young curate with acne-scarred face who had never heard her name and certainly never drank strong tea from her yellow china cups.

I'm sure, though, that Granny wasn't upset; and she must have smiled from Heaven as the prayers were said.

Gracious and completely understanding . . . as always.

# about the author

JOAN COMISKEY was born in Brooklyn, N.Y. to Irish immigrant parents, but was raised and educated from infancy in a small rural village in southern Ireland. After leaving Ireland in her early 20s, she worked for several years in nursing in England. Then, while working as a ship's nurse, she came "home" to America, landing in New York in 1960. She began writing as a teenager, but over the years had sometimes written more "in her head." Now, in her "golden" years, she has gathered together some of those writings, capturing and sharing some of the special memories of her Irish childhood.

# acknowledgments

To my husband Vincent, without whose unwavering support, insight, encouragement, and love, none of the pieces would have been completed. I am grateful to early readers of the memories as they evolved over many years. Finally, I want to acknowledge my debt to Claudia Sammartino. Her editorial and publishing skills were absolutely essential. I am honored and proud to have had her expert care and input.

Made in the USA
Charleston, SC
06 April 2014